MW00944372

AMAZON FBA MASTERY COACHING

THE DEFINITIVE GUIDE TO LEARN THE SECRET WAY TO SELL FULFILLMENT BY AMAZON

How to Launch a Private Label and Earn Six Figures of Passive Income in an Easy Step-By-Step Method from Total Beginners to Really Advanced

JONATHAN FITZPATRICK

AMAZON FBA MASTERY COACHING

Copyright © 2019 by Jonathan Fitzpatrick.

For information contact :

Suite #K231125

13820 NE Airport Way

Portland, OR, 97251

United States

info@jonathanfitzpatrickauthor.com

www.jonathanfitzpatrickauthor.com

www.facebook.com/jonathanfitzpatrickau
thor

First Edition: April 2019

SIGN UP

Visit my website www. *jonathanfitzpatrickauthor.com* and enter your email address in the sign-up form to receive free exclusive bonus contents related to the updates of this book and find out everything about Jonathan Fitzpatrick's new publications, launch offers and other exclusive promotions!

DISCLAIMER

The information contained in this book is for general information and educational purposes only.
This book assumes no responsibility for errors or omissions in the contents on the Service.

This book have no liability for any damage or loss (including, without limitation, financial loss, loss of profits, loss of business or any indirect or consequential loss).

 JONATHAN FITZPATRICK

CONTENTS

Introduction

My name is Jonathan Fitzpatrick and I am an online entrepreneur. In my first 12 months of business, I was able to go from earning $0 to earning six-figures of passive income through Amazon FBA. Now I want to share my knowledge and experience with others so that they can also reach their full potential. Learn how to launch a private label and earn six-figures of passive income in just twelve months! This comprehensive guide applies whether you are an experienced seller or just getting started.

I'm writing this introduction from the first class cabin of a flight bound for Tokyo as it is going to be a long flight, and I intend to make the best out of my time. Whether you take me for my word, or not, I can assure you that this vacation is entirely funded by my FBA account. While still on vacation, I will still be running my business if necessary. It completely runs on my smart phone, laptop and sometimes the bar-code scanner.

More so, you would be envious of the amount of freedom I have to juggle and balance my personal and professional life. When was the last time I did something I love and enjoy? Well, I currently am. I love writing and disseminating knowledge. But if you are speaking in the realms of hobbies, then you should know that I do not miss any of my evening book club sessions. In fact, just yesterday afternoon I managed to attend a painting class, grab a drink with a friend and still managed to be home on time to read my niece a bedtime story. I believe that now I have your undivided attention.

These are the perks that have come with FBA. Fulfillment By Amazon. This is the gold mine that is little understood by those who know about it, let alone less publicized to the general public. For those who are quite familiar with the service, they understand that it is as simple as Buy; Ship;

Receive Payment. Then why is it so complicated if it seems as natural.

Well, truth be told, FBA is rather intensive. Regardless of Amazon handling a huge chunk of the program, the bit left to the sellers is not a walk in the park. But I suppose that you already know this, and that is precisely why you are here. You understand what it takes to achieve your financial goals. With your primary goals set out, it will be a far easier job wading through these waters. Add that to an active and fueled mindset and a prosperous story is already being penned.

This book is meant to give an in depth understanding of Fulfillment By Amazon and how to reap maximum benefits from it. It provides instructions and guidelines for managing an FBA business as well as tips to give you an edge over your competition. I have learned most of the practices through research, experimentation, trial, and error, consulting other FBA sellers and personally through patience. FBA, the book, has been compiled to help you achieve success through Amazon. Do you wish to make a couple of thousand dollars in monthly profits? Well, roll up your sleeves, it is time for business.

Tip: I would like you to take a moment and reflect on your mindset. It is the one thing that will keep you going. Set it right, and no obstacle will deter you from that handsome Amazon deposit in your bank account.

Chapter 1: FBA Basics

Fulfillment by Amazon (FBA) is often considered a subset of the dropshipping industry with a few major differences. Whereas with traditional dropshipping a third party is responsible for the sourcing and fulfilment of the orders, merchants in a Fulfilment by Amazon relationship send their items to Amazon who is then responsible for storing and shipping the items in question in return for a portion of the profits from the sale of the item. If you have an item that you are interested in creating a private label for but you weren't sure where the items were going to be stored or how you were going to find time to fill all of your future orders, then FBA is the answer.

In addition to making the physical transaction part of an online sale much less of a hassle, those who participate in the FBA program also get preferential treatment when it comes to search results as well as how their packages are shipped. Amazon power users who take advantage of the Amazon Prime membership option receive free 2-day shipping on countless products that Amazon sells directly, but also, on all of the items sold by those in the FBA program.

This means that by simply signing up for FBA you are already placing your future products at a huge advantage when compared to similar products that you will one day be competing against. The amount you are charging for shipping will also affect your Amazon rating in several ways, but suffice it to say, a lower shipping cost is always better. This, coupled with 2-day shipping, goes a long way towards creating positive mindshare, even if your product costs a little more, or is of a new private label brand that the customer has not yet heard of.

How it works

FBA works by allowing sellers to send their products directly to the nearest Amazon fulfilment facility where the products are then stored until they are sold. You then have the option of paying for additional preparation or labeling services as required while paying a monthly storage fee based on the amount of space your products require. Then, once a customer finds them online, Amazon takes care of all of the fulfilment tasks, including the all-important customer service and returns portion of the process which a more traditional dropshipping service would leave up to you.

It is important to understand just how valuable the fact that Amazon is fulfilling the orders in question is, especially when it comes to private label products from a new company. The Amazon name carries quite a bit of weight with customers, and having that name involved in the transaction will make them much more likely to go ahead and pull the trigger on the transaction in question. While they will hopefully become a loyal follower of your brand someday, being an FBA member gets you in the door. Studies show that FBA sellers typically see as much as a 30 percent boost in sales compared to more traditional sellers.

In return for the perks, FBA members pay a $40 monthly fee as well as a percentage of the sale price of each item. You will also be required to pay fees related to the weight of the item when it comes to shipping, any handling fees, pack or pick fees and storage fees based on the square footage. Additionally, you will be required to pay fees related to individually labeling all of your products as you will not want them commingled with other similar products as this will only dilute your brand. If you are unsure if this fee structure will fit the private label products, you may be hoping to one day sell you can check out the revenue calculator available on the official FBA site to determine if your idea is likely going to be a success.

When it comes to fleshing out your business plan it is important to factor in the benefits in terms of exposure that you will likely receive as well as any costs you might incur. This is especially true if you are going to be creating your own product line as you are going to need all of the potential customers you can get. If your initial idea does not appear as though it is going to work with FBA, you may want to consider alternative types of products as the solution is out there, you just have to do the work and find it.

A private label brand is any brand that it is not owned by a major company or organization. Over the past 20 years, private label brands have seen nearly double the growth of more mainstream brands, and the growth in niche markets where the importance of individual ingredient lists is much higher; much like customer interest levels when it comes to getting to know the creators of unique brands.

This is in large part due to the greater amount of perceived control that goes along with these types of products and it is something you can use to your advantage if marketed properly. What's more, when you decide to create your own private label you will have complete control over the branding and marketing of the product in question, allowing you to create something truly special that speaks directly to your target audience. Additionally, you will have the added advantage of perceived value as you don't have to deal with all of the added waste that comes from working with a major brand.

The Product
For me personally, this is the most difficult part of starting a business. The beginning. The

foundation, perhaps. Knowing what to sell to people is like knowing the exact shirt and tie combination to wear for a specific job interview. A polished cover letter and rehearsed answers for the interviewer's questions are far less effective if you dress inappropriately. Too casual is disrespectful and too formal makes you look desperate.

The items you choose to sell to people say something about you. Regardless of whether or not you have any practical use for the product, your signature will be all over them (sometimes literally). The material quality, the packaging, the storage conditions, the handling. While a one-time customer may not notice a lot of those things, a regular customer will likely be looking at all of those things and more.

Choosing a product: If you did not start your business with a creative idea of your own already in mind then you will need to look for an opportunity. Any of the following is a great place to start

- Opportunities in Keywords
- Building an Interesting Brand
- Identify and Solve a Pain Point
- Identify and Cater to Passions
- Look for an Opportunity Gap
- Utilize Your Own Experience
- Capitalize on Trends
- Opportunities in Keywords

Keywords: Starting from the top, we have opportunities derived from search engine keywords. Keywords are the words and phrases that users type into a search engine. Knowing a little bit about search engine optimization (SEO) is essential if you want to be competitive online. A lot of business owners are willing to handsomely pay savvy individuals to manage their advertising campaigns.

Anyway, the idea here is to find keywords that have a high search volume (a lot of people looking for it) and low competition (few good matches). That right there is a golden opportunity. Giving the people something that they already want means you can launch with a smaller ad campaign than if you were trying to get into a competitive market.

Building an interesting brand: A popular strategy for entering a saturated and/or competitive market, as the 'new kid on the block' you have less money, less influence, and less experience than the older boys. Trying to keep up with them is an almost futile act. You need something unique. Something that only you have that makes others pay attention to you even if you are a rookie in a room full of champions and veterans. This is your brand.

I could list some specific examples but there are just so many! I suppose one of the most well-known is Apple's more stylish branding being used to separate their products from Microsoft's dull ones. Even a Goliath like Microsoft is not safe from an opponent who knows how to stand out from the rest.

You can take the same route as Apple and distinguish your brand visually. You could also just tell your own story. Few consumers think about the people behind brands like Wal-Mart or McDonald's. Instead, they think of how huge those businesses are and how rich the owners and executives must be. Highlighting your status as a small business without a lot of capital can make you far more relatable to the average shopper.

Identify and solve a pain point: There has never been a better time to be alive in history. The best and brightest of us have worked diligently to make every one of us live comfortably. Once deadly diseases are now treatable if not curable. Modern vehicles make travel so easy that plans are being made to explore the solar system. Advancing technology continues to make performing tasks so easy that people are afraid of not having jobs in the near future.

All of the things that cause discomfort are pain points. I mentioned some big ones but there are small ones, too. I can type out this book on a computer because dipping pens in ink that smudged all over the paper was a pain point for writers. The printing press and typewriters were revolutionary even though they were not cures for cancer. Try isolating some minor frustrations and then think of products that can remove them.

Note that when I brought up advancing technology I also included a fear that people have. The solution to what was once a problem can create a new problem. Be on the lookout for innovations that change the way a lot of us live. Those changes can create an environment for a new pain point to develop.

Identify and cater to passions: I think this type of opportunity is the easiest to understand. You identify something that a lot of people are interested and provide an additional something that appeals to those people. This is what many people do with blogs and vlogs to start building a following. Someone who wants to travel but is unable to will settle for a virtual escape in the meantime.

Fan merchandise falls under this category, too. You should get permission before reproducing symbols and logos that belong to someone else, but fan art can be sold legally as of the time that I am writing this. If you are an artist, slap that art onto clothes, mugs, and bags if you think the fanatics will buy them.

Not an artist? Well somebody has to supply all the clothes, mugs, and bags to be printed over. Creative types are all about that passion and you can take advantage of that. It is also possible that one person can do all of the above. If you share the same passion as your clients then a lot of this work could feel more like an addictive hobby. Cater responsibly.

Look for an opportunity gap: As smartphones became ubiquitous in the early 2000s, the people ran into a problem. They wanted to take photos of themselves using their phones. However, it was near impossible to get the right angle and lighting while holding the device only an arm's length away. Friendly bystanders were a godsend but could not be relied upon at all times. The people cried out for a solution and the market answered their cries with the Selfie Stick.

That is how you take advantage of an opportunity gap. Human beings always want 'more' regardless of how much they already have. People in houses want bigger houses. People who own a car want another car. People who get food delivered to their homes want faster delivery. There will always be a demand for something new to make living just a little bit easier. Provide something to achieve that goal and you will have plenty of business.

Opportunity gaps are like minor pain points; nobody complains because they are more of an inconvenience than a cause of stress. Discovering one will take research and awareness. You can ask the people around you about the products they use and if they feel like something is missing when they use them.

Utilize your own experience: Young entrepreneurs are still young people. They are optimistic and ambitious with little to lose and so much to gain. Older people tend to move with caution and lower expectations. One of your biggest assets, as you age, is your experience. Wisdom cannot be bought or stolen and its value is priceless.

The more work experience and expertise you have in a field, the more of an advantage you have others who are entering it. Writing and publishing your own book should not only generate some income but also show others in the field that you know what you are talking about. As a consequence of that, any products you sell in the future will stand out because of your reputation.

Your choice of media does not have to be in writing. You can make videos or host seminars. The objective is just to make it known that you are an authority in your field. Not feeling confident? Do it regardless! If even one of your industry insights is unique it might be enough to establish a following.

Capitalize on trends: This one is tricky. The idea is similar to that of finding opportunities in keywords. A trend has to be identified early and capitalized on immediately for the best results. Being the second person to catch on might not be good enough depending on consumer demand and how long the trend lasts.

Let us pretend that I have identified what I believe to be a trend. How do I confirm this? The most straightforward way is to buy a small amount of whatever I think I need to sell and put it up for sale.

If sales are anything less than stellar then either I am too late or I have not identified a trend at all. If it really is trendy I should see a significant amount of that product sold in a couple of days. The next step is to buy a lot more of that trendy product and make sure consumers know what I have done so.

Consider different types of products

For starters, you are going to want to ensure that the first products in your inaugural product line are durable enough to stand up to a bumpy delivery process as nothing will ruin your ratings like numerous reviews talking about how their purchases arrived broken

Choose the right items: While it is natural to consider big ticket items to flip as an easy way of generating a major payout, the fact of the matter is that you are almost always going to have more luck selling numerous small items than you will selling one large item. The best place to start is with common, everyday items that you know someone, somewhere is sure to need.

The goal here should be to choose items that are always going to be in demand, but not those that are so vital as to ensure that most people are likely to run out and buy it the second they need it, no matter what the circumstances. While not the most exciting advice, give it a try and you will see that a hefty supply of printer cartridges or diapers can be worth their long-term weight in gold.

While certain items are going to be worthwhile investments no matter what the situation, others can be sure to generate massive windfalls if picked up for the right price to start with. A great example of this is holiday decorations as they can easily be picked up for bargain basement pricing starting the day after the holiday in question has passed. Keep in mind, however, that you can only realistically expect to make a profit on these types of items if you have the time and inclination to hold on to them until the next year when that holiday once again rolls around. Alternatively, you can keep up to date on the bleeding edge of cool and purchase items that are sure to be in high demand six months down the line for much more reasonable prices.

Choosing the right items to sell also means considering all facets of the items in question, including how easy they will ultimately be to ship once you do, in fact, make a sale. Failing to do so leaves you open to the possibility of having to deal with a large number of returns on items that are needlessly fragile. Along similar lines, it is also extremely important to consider the overall weight of the item in question to ensure that shipping costs aren't going to be eating up too much of your profit as well as any issues if you are going to ship the product internationally.

Start selling

Now that you are ready, it is time to go to Amazon and set up your seller account. To begin with, you should set up a free Individual Seller Plan. As you do this, you will want to be sure that you are verifying your account information. Before we go over upgrading to FBA, we suggest understanding the difference between the selling plans. This may sway your thoughts on joining FBA.

Individual Selling Plan
- $0.99 for each item that sells on Amazon
- Only one listing at a time
- Includes both online listings as well as the management of your orders
- Includes Seller Central tools to help with account functions

Professional Selling Plan
- Costs a Monthly Fee of $39.99
- Get multiple listings by using uploads and spreadsheets
- Includes reports and fees on your inventory and management of orders
- Includes access to the Amazon Marketplace Web Service, API functions, and daily reports on your store's performance.

If you decide that FBA is the proper choice for your store, you can quickly switch your selling plan. To begin, you will want to click on the tab that says 'Seller Account.' Once you have done this, tap on the settings button and click 'Account Info.' Under this tab, it will ask you to click a button that says 'Modify Plan.' Once you are here, you will be able to upgrade your plan, and you are all set to go! The program processes immediately. It should be noted that you will be charged a $0.99 fee for any orders that you close. From this point on, you will be charged $39.99 a month as long as you keep the Professional plan.

Amazon Seller's Application: The first thing that you will want to do is to download the seller application available from Amazon directly. This application is extremely useful as it allows you to put in the details of any product you are thinking about selling to learn how much you will make off of the item at a set price minus all the various fees that will come along with it. What's more, this application will allow you to see how many other people are currently selling the same item, as well as which varieties of a given brand are the most popular among consumers at the current point in time.

CamelCamelCamel.com: This website and other like it allow you to find out more detailed information regarding how a specific product is currently doing on Amazon. These types of sites provide you with the data that you will need to not only determine if the price an item is currently selling for is on the high or low end of the spectrum, it will show you the entire history of that item so you know if you have found an emerging trend or have latched on to a product that is past its prime. Checking out this site or other like it, before you set your prices, is extremely important to ensure you aren't accidentally selling yourself, and your items, short.

Listing items

When it comes to listing the items that you have worked so hard to create or buy for a price that you can turn a profit on the first thing you are going to want to do is find the Inventory option at the top of the page in the Amazon Seller Central page. From there all you need to do is select the option to add a product. After this, you will want to select the option to create a new product which will require the use of a unique UPC code as well as an AISN number, the specifics of which can be found below.

After you have created the item that you are planning to list, you will be asked 3 important questions. First you will need to set a price for the item, then you will need to describe the condition of the items you are selling and finally, you will want to choose the Fulfilment by Amazon option which is listed as wanting Amazon to take care of shipping. When it comes to choosing a price for your products, a good rule of thumb is to start out by looking at similar products in your niche and then setting a comparative price. It is important to take into account your costs as well, as underselling the competition won't do any good if you aren't making a profit in the long run.

Creating a shipping plan: After you have finished loading in all of your products, you will want to choose the option to Send Inventory on the final product. This will lead to a prompt to create a shipping plan which includes choosing a shipping address and packaging type. Packaging type can be split into 2 different categories, individual products or case-packed products. In general, you are likely going to want to select case-packed products which indicates that all of the items in each box are the same. Shipping your products in groups will save you plenty of logistical headaches in the long run and is always recommended.

After you have finished choosing your shipping plan you will be prompted to determine which items you are going to be shipping at this time. Adding products to the shipment is as easy as clicking the add product button. If you find yourself in need of adding additional items, simply post them as normal before selecting the option to add the item to an existing plan.

Shipping your items: Once you have all of the items added to the shipping plan in question you will want to go back to the main Seller Central page before selecting the option for Inventory. From there you will want to select the option to "continue shipping plan" where you will be able to list how many of each product you are going to be sending. If your product is going to require some type of preparation prior to being sent to customers this is also where you make it clear what all you are going to need Amazon to do to get them ready to ship.

You will also need to reconfirm that you are going to require labeling services before being asked to set the weight of the package or packages in question. This doesn't need to be exact, as long as you estimate over what you know the weight to be. This can quickly become costly, however, so investing in a package scale is recommended.

From there it is simply a matter of boxing up your products, printing out the provided shipping labels and dropping the boxes off at a local UPS location. Your products will be listed live as soon as they reach the nearest Amazon fulfillment office and then it will be up to your ancillary marketing activities as well as your becoming an authority, discussed in the next chapter, to get your products sold as quickly as possible.

Subscriptions: Amazon subscriptions are new to Amazon and they were launched in order to help customers save money and for sellers to get more money. With this, you are going to get a discount because there are going to be a variety of products that are going to arrive on the customer's doorstep on a schedule.

This helps to convince customers, since items that they need to buy regularly are going to be sent to their store and this makes it to where they do not have to worry about going to the warehouse and the store not having the brand that they want or the see that the price has gone up without them knowing.
Like anything else on Amazon, the product that you have to sell is going to have to comply with the

rules of Amazon as well as the rules and regulations of the territory that you are in. These rules and regulations are in place to ensure that the customers and the sellers are protected.

Not only do you have the option of doing a subscription that is delivered to the customer's door, but you can do subscriptions on Amazon Prime, Amazon TV, and Kindle Unlimited. All of these are brilliant strategies to use when selling the product that you have to offer. It all depends on what you are selling.

Chapter 2: Choose the Right Niche

When it comes to ensuring you are ultimately able to market the products you eventually sell as effectively as possible the first, and perhaps most important, thing that you will need to consider is what niche of the market you are going to cater to. A niche is a specialized section of the larger consumer market as a whole which naturally lends itself to a specific set of customer demographics as well as products and interests. For example, the online dating market is a broad category which holds several different niches including things like polyamory, green dating, sacred sexuality, soulmates and more. These niches can then be broken down even further into things such as polyamory over 40 or homosexual sacred sexuality.

Choosing a
specialized
niche is a
great way
to help
yourself
stick out
from the
crowd and,
in so
doing,
making
your FBA
business
that
much more
profitable in the long run. This is
easier said than done, however,
as not every niche or sub-niche is
going to be profitable for one
reason or another which is why it
is so important to do the proper
research before you begin.
Remember, once you have
branded your store with a specific
niche it can be extremely difficult
to change it later on.

The best way to make a lot of
money is for your niche to be
something you care about enough

to go back to every day. This is going to drive you to work on it and constantly produce something new. If you don't care about your niche then it's going to show through in your posts. You can expect some amount of return, but they will almost certainly not be great. Bear that in mind as you go forward.

So, you've gotten to the point now that you want to start considering an FBA business in a serious way then the first thing that you're going to need to do is pick your niche. There are two ways to go about doing this.

The first is the hardest: go off of your passions. If you do this, you're going to have to find innovative ways using products that affiliate companies offer, if they don't have any for your specific niche. However, this can pay off by you making really creative and potentially viral posts using things in unconventional ways that people will see as super intriguing. This is a good way to bring in a whole bunch of people.

In order to do this, you're going to need to be very crafty and keep an eye on what's available. Additionally, a lot of your income will be coming through other means mentioned in this book rather than affiliate marketing. However, it's an option worth considering because affiliate marketing can almost certainly play a part in a strategy like this one.

The second is the easiest, but you're playing chance in two respects. The second method is to simply see what products and avenues are available to you through affiliate marketing channels and then derive your niche from that. In some cases, this will intertwine with the first concept and you'll find something that you're both passionate about and that there are a fair number of products for which you can market. However, this won't always be the case.

In the event that you can't find something you're reasonably passionate about, simply try to find something that you're somewhat interested in or would like to learn more about for yourself. This will make it easier to research and find topics related to it that you're interested in.

However, sometimes you just won't be able to find anything that interests you. In these cases, you can still just go with whatever you think would do fairly well. Sometimes intuition can be a really important thing, and in these cases, you should just trust your intuition in trying to find a pertinent niche through affiliate marketing channels.

The last and third most prominent way to figure out your niche is simply to use keywords in order to learn what topics are hot right now. This might give you the most instantaneous benefit, but you will inevitably find it rather difficult to carry this out for a long period of time because trends are constantly changing. You'll most likely find success using this method in the short run (if you can write some great articles and take advantage of available affiliate marketing opportunities) but you'll find it difficult to maintain that same level of success in the long run.

If you do decide to take this avenue, however, all you'll have to do is get access to popular keywords and figure out what's trending. The easiest way to do this is probably to take advantage of Google Trends. Simply Google "google trends hot trends" and the page you're looking for should be relatively easy to find. This will tell you the most trending topics of the day every hour or so. It's generally the top 20.

However, this can be rather unwieldy as it won't exactly tell you the sort of information you're wanting to write a book about. After all, these are just the most trending searches for the last day or so, and they generally on very specific people and events rather than topics you can easily write a book about.

Narrowing down a niche

Choose the right target: When it comes to finding the best possible niche or subniche for you, the first thing you are going to want to consider is who your ideal target audience is going to be. There are several different options when it comes to choosing the right audience, starting with choosing the one of which you are currently a part. This has the added bonus of ensuring you don't have to do excessive research to get started and will also ensure that you have the interest required to stick with it in the long-term.

Alternately, you could choose a niche that you are just starting to become more interested in, though in doing so you run the risk of losing interest in the topic and being stuck with a blog you are loath to update. If you can't seem to come up with the right audience, but you have a niche in mind then you can simply start with the niche and seek out an audience based on the ideal characteristic, discretionary spending.

Learn more about them: Once you have a target audience in mind, the next thing you are going to need to do is to think about all of the problems, challenges, pain points, aspirations and desires that your target audience likely deals with on a regular basis and how you can make this process easier for them in as many different ways as possible. A good place to go for research at this juncture is a basic Google search as if you put in problems your target audience deals with you will find searches revolving around ways to solve the problem. Without a problem to solve, the target audience will likely need to buy far less than they otherwise would.

Find the profit: After you find a few problems that people are regularly looking to solve, the next thing you are going to want to do is to determine which are going to be the most profitable from an affiliate marketing standpoint. The best way to do so is going to be by going to Adwords.Google.com and looking up the keyword planning tool. This tool will allow you to filter the search results you see to just those that you are interested in before searching for both local and global results.

Determine if anything is going to set you apart from the pack: Depending on what you find during your initial fact finding mission your next step will need to be figuring out just what is going to set you and your products apart from all of the other stores that are offering similar, if not the same product. What this typically comes down to is how much personality or added value you can add to your store, to the point that it makes it preferable for customers to seek you out instead of simply settling for a generic version and calling it a day.

People seek out niche options despite the fact that Amazon sells practically everything because they like knowing they are directly connecting with another person and because they are looking for a little extra personality in their purchased goods. If you can't afford to throw in additional incentives, consider specializing in a few items to a degree that other stores, even your competitors, can't match. Regardless of how specific your competitors might be, there is general a way to be more specialized, consider the market from other perspectives and you will find your own way to shine.

Check out magazines: While magazines largely make their money through the subscriptions that their readers pay, another essential way that these magazines make their money is through the products that they promote. For example, if you have ever flipped through a magazine and have thought that there are far too many advertisements in it, then it is safe to say that the magazine that you are looking gets a lot of money from the advertisements that they feature. While this fact may mean that you have too many pages to flip through to get to some readable content, it also means that from a research perspective, this magazine may benefit you more than you think. Remember, these advertisers would not be buying ad spots in magazines if they did not think that the ads would lead to sales.

Another important tip that goes along with looking through the advertisements that you see in ads is to be on the lookout for ads that are enticing to you personally. While yes, a business should be as emotionless as possible, your dropshipping business should also sell products about which you are somewhat passionate. For

example, if you decide that you are
going to sell tires online because
your research suggests that they
will sell well, but you hate cars in
general, then this may not be the
best option for you. If you can find
a happy medium between a
product that will profitable and a
product that you will also enjoy
selling, that would be ideal. Of
course, if your goal is to make as
much money as you can, then this
advice may be lost on you;
however, it can be argued that
enjoying what you are doing
should be a part of any business
endeavor that you take on.

Check on the competition: Once
you have an idea of what items are
in need in the niche, your next step
should be to determine the level of
competition when it comes to
specific item types. The more
online stores that you find selling
the same product or variations
thereon the more direct
competition you will have when it
comes time to actually start selling
products. You can find more than
2 pages of search results selling

the items you are thinking about selling with no more than a basic search you may want to consider a different niche or at least targeting a sub-niche to carve out more of a unique audience.

While checking out the competition you will want to do all of the reconnaissance to ensure that you have a good idea of what their product turnover seems to be and how robust their customer base seems to be. While scouting out the competition it is important to approach them in a rational fashion and not set out determined to crush them no matter what. At this point is likely a better choice to cut your losses and find another niche before you start putting real time and effort into this one; remember, discretion is the better part of valor.

Additionally, you will want to consider the strength of any obvious competitor's social media campaigns and search engine optimization SEO. To determine how popular and effective each is, you simply need to do basic searches with terms related to the niche you are interested in infiltrating. If a few names keep coming up again and again and again, then you may want to consider looking for a new product to sell.

Maintain perspective: If your first niche ends up looking as though it is already as crowded enough as it is, then it is important to not stay married to an idea that you have absolutely no investment in at this point. It is much better to find out that your first choice ended up not being as viable as you thought in the planning stage rather than when you have already made a significant investment into making your online store a reality. Maintain the right perspective and be ready to walk away up to the point that your website is live and ready to receive customers.

Consider the quality: When it comes to finding ways to set yourself apart from the competition, one of the best ways of doing so is by offering a better quality of product for relatively the same price. Depending on the types of items you are selling, being known for quality is more important than anything save an extreme price difference.

When given a choice the average consumer is likely to put quality first in terms of importance which is why you must ensure that whatever you end up selling you do whatever you need to in order to ensure that the quality of every product that your store sells be as high as possible. While it may be tempting to reduce your costs as thoroughly as possible early on, in reality, this is less of an investment in the future and more of a guarantee that your first customers could be your only customers. A reputation for quality will spread quickly and can do more for a fledgling startup than just about any other marketing tool.

Chapter 3: Products

Once you have gone ahead and chosen what niche you want to fill, the next thing you need to do is determine what you want to sell. Deciding what you sell is extremely important as it will influence the type of marketing you will want to try further down the line and also determine where you can go to source the things you want to sell. In general, you want items that are specific enough to not already have thousands of online stores already filling the niche, while at the same time broad enough to still see traffic from general Google searches. The right mix can be tricky, but you'll know it when you find it.

Consider the demand: One of the first things you will want to consider is whether you have the knowledge about your chosen niche that is currently being underserved by the online community. For example, if you really enjoy knitting and know that alpaca wool yarn is the best, then consider selling it if it is relatively hard to find currently. Everyone is part of a niche if you try hard enough, take the time to think about the items you buy regularly that are either hard to find or wear out extremely quickly, it can help to write the ideas down as you think of them, so you don't need to work through the entire process with each, ruining your brainstorming flow.

Once you have a list of ideas, the next step is to assess the relative demand for each of the potential items in question. As long as the items you are thinking about selling aren't extremely obscure, this process should be relatively straightforward. A good way to start researching the popularity of a specific item is to simply type it into the Google search bar and see what options appear under the autofill option. Again, what you are looking for here is a demand that is not being entirely met, so questions about where to find specific items are a great positive unmet desire indicator.

___

Private label basics

When it comes to creating your own private label there are a few things you are going to want to keep in mind to ensure you get into the private label FBA business with the proper mindset. This means that the first thing you need to consider is the amount of capital that it is going to require in order to create your initial product line. It requires a significant amount of capital to get your own private label up and running and the larger or more complicated your product is the greater those expenses are going to be. If you are interested in getting started selling on Amazon on the cheap, retail arbitrage is more your speed, to create a private label you have to be willing to spend.

The next thing you need to understand is that creating a private label is not going to make you large amounts of money in a fashion that is either quick or easy. Instead, it is going to take lots of hard work and dedication and be unlikely to pay off realistically for anywhere between 6 months and a year depending on various factors related to the niche you ultimately chose. For those who choose to stick it out, however, the rewards are substantial. Not only will you have a fully functioning brand operating exclusively through Amazon but you will have something that businesses all around the world are constantly striving for, brand recognition, and it will be yours and yours alone.

Deciding if your product is a good fit for a private label: Once you've done some research and determined what niche is going to likely be a good fit for you, the next thing you are going to want to consider is if the market is favorable when it comes to private labels. The first thing this means is determining if there is one or more national brand in the niche space that already dominates the

space. This means you will
naturally be limited in what you
can choose, though you can likely
find a sub niche that is more
agreeable to private labels if you
try hard enough.

Design the right logo: When it
comes to designing a logo, it is
important to consider what you
ultimately go with long and hard
as your logo is going to be seen
more than any other aspect of
your business. When it comes to
finding the right logo for you, a
good place to start is with
common symbols as when done
properly your logo will spring to
mind whenever that symbol is
used. When thinking about your
logo it is important to consider
how it looks when it is the size of a
thumbnail as it is when it is filling
your screen completely. You never
know where your logo might end
up and it is important to plan
accordingly. Likewise, it is
important to pick a logo that can
default to colors that resemble the
colors of your store but it should
be just as recognizable when any

other colors are inserted into the mix.

When choosing a logo, it is important to pick something that is timeless instead of cashing in on a current trend. While a trendy logo might get you some notice today, it is much more likely to be a hindrance in the long run. Create a logo that you are sure will be comfortable with for the foreseeable future.

When it comes to choosing the colors, the first thing you should consider is a few core colors that complement one another as well as few more colors that are variations on the first. It is important to keep the color variation to a minimum as simple, clean looks are currently in fashion. Certain colors are also known to stimulate certain responses which make them natural choices when it comes to selling certain products.

Choosing a name: While it doesn't take much to pick out a bad company name when you see it, understand what it takes to create a good name can be much more complicated. To get started, you may want to consider which of the three primary name conventions, whimsical, evocative or descriptive, that you want to explore more fully. Descriptive names are self-explanatory, much like the names themselves and include things like Office Depot, Bed, Bath and Beyond and Home Depot. Alternately you can go with something that is evocative without really being descriptive such as Warby Parker or Oracle. Finally, you may want to consider something that's catchy without being meaningful such as Twitter, Google or Hulu.

Know what's popular: When it comes to creating a useful business name, it will automatically make it easier for you to attract new customers if people can find your business by simply searching for whatever product or service it is that you provide. The best way to go about picking out the optimal search terms for your product or service is to utilize the website UberSuggest.org. All you need to do is enter any word into its search bar and it will provide you with all of the most popular search terms related to it.

Consider related words: If you don't have anything catchy in mind right off the bat, the first thing you are going to want to consider is words that are naturally related to the product or service that you want to provide. A thesaurus of either the physical or digital sort is a great place to start and you never know when a new word might spark the creative notion that gives birth to your new business name. If nothing jumps out at you right from the start, simply make a list of between 50 and 100 potential options and save them for later.

Product Manufacturing

This section applies to those of you who want to make your own products or even have an invention manufactured.

Prototype: The first step in the manufacturing process is to create a prototype. The prototype is going to be the preliminary model of the product that you want to be made in bulk. If you are creating something mechanical then the prototype has to be able to function exactly as you want it to. Otherwise, you could manufacture hundreds of models that are

effectively   overpriced
paperweights.

It is safe to say that creating your own style of t-shirt is different from re-inventing the electric oven.

Some prototypes are things that you can make yourself while others will require that you hire some help. Unless time and resources are things you have in abundance, it would be smart to do all of the necessary research before building the prototype. Very rarely will you be satisfied with the first attempt but having a good place to start will make the process easier going forward.

Location: Once you have a working prototype, you have to decide whether you want it to be made domestically or overseas. For this example, I will assume that you live in the United States. Some products are only made in the United States so there is no decision to make in those instances. For others, you must consider the benefits and costs.

Manufacturing your product in the United States means that lead times, the time between the beginning and end of the production process, will be relatively short for any location in the country. Additionally, the quality of your product will be easier to maintain and improve. You can also advertise that your products are made in the United States which a lot of consumers will be happy to know.

Outsourcing your production overseas means a drop in quality control, but at a much better price. A plastic product can be manufactured in China for less than half the price quoted by an American manufacturer. However, lead times will be much higher. You could pay significantly more for express shipping but then that defeats the purpose of doing business overseas.

As a general rule, manufacture your product domestically if you want hundreds of copies and in foreign countries if you want thousands. Look into having a representative from your country manage production overseas. The cost of hiring that person is worth preventing the possibility that you receive five thousand devices that are all dysfunctional.

Quoting the product: So you have a prototype and you know where you want to have it produced. Now it is time to shop around. Send your sample to the factory that you want to work with and get an estimate for how much this work is going to cost you. Make sure when comparing quotes from different factories that the quotes are identical. The same quantities, the same materials, the same custom fees. Everything included in one must also be included in the other. If not then you will have to comb through the quote with excess costs to get an accurate price comparison.

Quotes will include terms like FOB which means 'freight on board'. The letters FOB will be followed by a destination so you might see 'FOB New York'. That number will be the price quoted to you is for the goods to be delivered to a port in New York. If you see 'FOB China' then that means the price includes delivery to a port in China. To get those goods delivered to the United States you would then need the services of a customs broker and a freight forwarder.

Customs brokers are the middle-men who are licensed to clear goods through customs. There are also customs agents who are individuals who do the same job. Freight forwarders assemble, collect, and consolidate shipping and distribution of loads that are less than a full trailer. Talking to people in these firms will help you better understand what they do.

Creating your own products: Depending on the types of products you will be selling, you may be able to forgo any type of more traditional manufacturing scenario and instead simply create everything you are going to sell by yourself. There are three different types of manufacturing that you can consider, the first is known as made to stock, which is where you crate the products beforehand and then use your Shopify page as a type of digital showroom.

To ensure you don't overspend on supplies in this scenario it is important to have a clear idea of what the expected demand for your product is going to be. Producing more of a product than you need tends to promote a sale mentality which can severely affect your bottom line depending on the amount of overestimation that occurred. Alternatively, you do not want to underestimate the demand that your product might receive as having too little stock on hand if your shop becomes popular early on can severely curtail your earnings potential in both the short or long term.

Another type of manufacturing strategy is to advertise the fact that your products are made to order based on customer specifications. This type of manufacturing ensures a natural inventory control mechanism and ensure you do not need to worry too much about the demand in the short term, as long as there is a steady stream of work coming in. Unfortunately, this type of manufacturing strategy won't work for every product category as the level of personalization possible will not equal out to the amount of extra time the order is going to take to create. If you hope to make this type of manufacturing work for you, you will need to ensure the added time comes with an appropriate amount of added value.

When it comes to creating your own items successfully, your goal at every turn should be to minimize as much risk as possible. If you have too much of a supply your demand will drop and if you don't supply enough then you might not be able to recoup your costs. As such, the most important thing to do is come up with a realistic business plan and stick to it no matter what.

Chapter 4: Mistakes to Avoid

*N*ot creating expandable brands and product lines from the start: If you are planning to build a sustainable business brand, you will want a larger umbrella of products to expand your business in the long run. Pick primary products that have plenty of complimentary purchases or can be bundled together with other items. This way you can keep adding items to create a longer product line under your brand. For example, if you zero in on the electronic gadgets niche, you may have a whole bunch of accessories and replaceable parts to sell to under a single business brand.

Go with bundled products and multi-packs if you are looking to score really big with Amazon FBA. Single items that sell are unlikely to be competition free or low competition on Amazon. Almost all products that sell reasonably well have tons of merchants in the category. Also, profit on one item products is swallowed by Amazon fees. Unless you can find a sweet spot between a high-priced product that is also in demand and has low competition, you may not be able to achieve stellar results with single items.

Also, your woes will increase if Amazon sells the product. Unless you have a terrific edge, it is going to be hard to compete with Amazon. Bundling up products or creating multi-packs may require greater time or money. You need to source a variety of items and bundle them. However, it can be highly beneficial for long term profits.

Underestimating the holidays: As long as you are comfortable holding on to these items for roughly 10 months, the deals you can find on decorations during the days immediately after most major holidays can practically guarantee acceptable profit margins on nearly everything you can imagine. What's more, by waiting 10 months before sending them to Amazon, you minimize your storage costs while at the same time taking advantage of all the people who like to plan for the holidays early. Alternately, you can wait until just a few weeks prior to the holiday to post your products and raise the prices even more to grab customers who waited until the last second and as a result, don't care about the costs.

Not considering the demand up front: While selling niche items is a good choice, that doesn't mean every item is automatically going to be a winner. Once you have an idea of the general types of items you want to sell the next step is to assess the relative demand for each of the potential items in question. As long as the items you are thinking about selling aren't extremely obscure, this process should be relatively straightforward. A good way to start researching the popularity of a specific item is to simply type it into the Google search bar and see what options appear under the autofill option. Again, what you are looking for here is a demand that is not being entirely met, so questions about where to find specific items are a great positive unmet desire indicator.

Another good place to look is in the autocomplete results of search engines on websites like eBay or Etsy, places where people are already going to search for harder to find items. In fact, if you ultimately find that the community for buying and selling related items is particularly robust, you may wish to consider starting a store on one of these platforms yourself.

Not listing products the right way
Even though we are told time and time again not to judge a book by its cover, shopping on Amazon, and anywhere online in general, is quite the opposite. One of the vital aspects of any listing on Amazon is the title, which informs potential buyers what the product is all about.

- Add keywords to the title to help the product to rank when buyers search
- Incorporate brand name
- Incorporate the name of the product

Add any features that distinguish the item
- Its use
- Color
- Size

For instance, if you are selling a pacifier, an ideal title would look something similar to this: Deluxe Silicone Baby Pacifier – Easy for Parents – BPA Free – Set of 2 Pacifiers – Blue

Goals for an Amazon product title should do the following:
- Educate potential consumers about the product, even before they read the product page
- Add a few keywords to showcase the product and its use

Not taking full advantage of images: Another important aspect of the product details of items on Amazon is the images included in the listing. They can cause shoppers to click on your listing just because of the quality of the image. That's why you should spend a good amount of time to research images that are top-notch. Amazon product images should include:

- Showcase product size by having a human hold it

- Information images like charts

- Images that include features of the product and compare it to other similar items

- Images of your product being utilized

- The back label

- The item from all different angles

A great resource to find top-notch Amazon images for your listings that are also affordable is AMZDream.com.

Not using enough bullet points: If potential buyers fail to be swooned by your choice of title and images, bullet points are the next best thing to get a straightforward reaction. You have five spaces to include bullet points, but this doesn't mean you only have to use five words or even sentences. I personally use short paragraphs in each of those bullet points to home in on benefits and features of the item. Address common questions and objections as well. Use the first three points to showcase your products most pertinent features and use the other bullet points to answer common inquiries or customer objections.

Not pricing products properly:
Opt to sell private label products
that are priced above $10. Amazon
lists items priced below $10 as "Add On Items, which means buyers cannot purchase your item by itself.

They have to make additional purchases to be able to buy your product. Additionally, profit margins for products priced below $10 after deducting Amazon's fee can be rather low for building a lucrative, long-term business. You will need a very higher sales volume to witness recent returns. Ideally, pick products that sell in the range of $10-$30 for higher profit margins.

Few things will kill you like low cost products on Amazon unless you predict an unrealistically high sales volume. You may think inexpensive items carry less risk or are more frequently picked up by customers on impulse.

However, selling products for below $5 is not likely to be profitable even with a high sales volume or next to nothing sourcing price. The shipping cost (to Amazon's warehouse) and fees will leave you with a few pennies.

Not treating it like a business: While Amazon FBA is not the same as having your traditional website up and running where you sell products to people, you should still treat the time that you spend on Amazon FBA the same that you would like an e-commerce business. Even though using Amazon FBA allows you to move away from creating your website, this does not mean that you should not take Amazon FBA seriously. You can lose money through this platform if you're not accurate in your estimates or you're sloppy with your profit margin calculations.

Not doing enough research: Another tip that many Amazon FBA users miss is that they don't do research on the Amazon site itself before deciding which products they're going to sell. Even if you enjoy fishing, this does not necessarily mean that selling fishing poles on Amazon is a decision that is going to lead to profits. Look at what's selling the most frequently on Amazon, and take note of any markets that may look like they're being underrepresented.

Having too many similar products: Unlike the notion of a niche website that we've already discussed, you do not have to worry about keeping a product line that is similar when you're using Amazon FBA. Because your seller profile is not going to define the type of business that you're running, you have the freedom to pick and choose the products that you want to sell. This can be great for someone who is good at doing research on products within Amazon's website. By figuring out the profit margin that's possible from certain products that are on the market, you should be able to

make better financial decisions for
yourself and your business.

Chapter 5: Tips for Success

Free inventory from your house: In my house, and likely yours as well, there are those items that you have not been used, ever! Not since you bought it because it was on sale, or there was a discount on the commodity. You could have used it once and return to the furthest corner of your closet or kitchen cabinet; no matter the case, these items can be turned into cash or better, profit! All you have to do is ship them to Amazon for that to happen.

Go hunting! Look through your book shelves, not all books in your library you like them, get them out and create space for the series you have been dying to read in your house and also reduce clutter. Go into your cabinets in your kitchen, your kids (if you have any) rooms with their permission, of course, your room as well and get rid of anything that you do not use at all. Some items you can get will surprise you; as these items can be used to create profits on Amazon.

Take the initiative and involve your family, friends, and neighbor-if they are willing to do so-and use all these items to earn cash! It can be an excellent way to spend a weekend, go through your trash to make money.

Using dunnage for shipments: The stuff, either puffy or protective wrapper, which you use to wrap your load to protect them from touching the sides of your shipping box that is the definition of dunnage.

There are various things you can use to protect your items so that they can arrive safely to your customer without breakage. The commodities in the list below are things you are most likely going to have in your house already. You can use:

- A newspaper blanket
- A variety of small cardboard boxes for glass items

- From your online arbitrage purchases, you can use the air pillows in them
- Tie printed papers in your everyday plastic grocery bags. This is to protect your shipment from getting in contact with the newsprint.

Free boxes from grocery stores for shipment: At the beginning of your Amazon FBA business, there won't be the need for you to pay for delivery boxes as you might not have the cash for it or you want to save the money you have for something else. You can get shipping boxes for free from grocery stores, your neighbors who have moved recently, or your friends or colleagues that have moved as well as places that recycle their old boxes. This will save you tons of cash. Make sure you select the best boxes out of all those that are at your disposal.

From the grocery store, ask the employees or attendees when they are restocking their shelves if you can have some of the boxes they are using. They are likely to let you come and collect to your heart's content or even when they are restocking come and get the boxes from their aisles.

Lighter fluid to remove price stickers: When reusing shipment boxes, there is the likelihood of price stickers being on them. Removing them is one struggle you will have to endure if you are trying to save money, but getting rid of the sticker residue is another struggle all on its own. When it comes to dealing with the residue from price stickers lighter fluid will do the trick every time.

Be careful when handling the liquid, and this will guarantee the removal of the residue. The process is quite simple, and all you will require is a Scotty peeler to remove the labels. You can use a Ronsonol lighter fluid. To do this, you will:

- Pour some of the lighter fluid on the sticker residue you want to get rid off

- Wait for a few minutes, approximately 5 minutes before you can try and remove the labels
- Using your Scotty peeler, gently try and pry the tag off.

Free inventory from Freecycle.org: Join a group of your area on Freecycle Network to be able to see what people are getting rid of or giving away for free that you can use for your shipments. You might be shocked by the number of things that you can source using this network. I got board games- both used and new-; books, in boxes; kitchen appliances, among other things.

The way it works is:
- Claim an item on the Freecycle Network
- The owner will leave it on the front porch or sidewalk
- Go and collect your item!

And that's it! Fairly easy and straightforward. This makes it easy for you to coordinate with the owner as you will get to set a time that you will pass by to collect it.

Boxes from arbitrage purchases: To be honest, most of the sourcing that you do for this type of business is through online sourcing. This means that there will be shipments sent to you in boxes. Thus you can use these same boxes for your shipments to Amazon. But you have to go to be careful and remove all bar codes. This can be removed or covered up before you can use the UPS label or Amazon.

Productivity tools: There are times when you just need to have a nap without worrying over unnecessarily about the way your online store is doing or how the shipments are fairing or remember if you sent a reply to your customer's comment. Below are some productivity tools that can help you shave off some of that time:

- IFTTT (If This Then That): This is mainly used by sellers on Amazon or eBay.

The app is used to alert the sellers of when sales have been made, or stock has been added back into inventory, or it has been added elsewhere.

- Facebook News Eradicator: With various sellers mainly spending their time on this social media platform going through the different FBA groups, it can take much of your time without you realizing it. To help you with this, this eradicator cuts down your extension extremely low. It allows you not to spend so much time on the internet getting to know what all your sources on Amazon FBA are talking about or all seller community groups.
- Cleer Pro: is an online app for online arbitrage. It is a software that makes it easier for you as a vendor to browse easily when

trying to look for deals, items or doing your research on Amazon.com

- Gmail Canned Responses: typing a similar response over and over again can get exhausting, and no one wants that kind of stress. Therefore, this app allows you to formulate a response that is going to reply automatically to the type of replies that come from your customers. The same app can be used to respond to an email you get in your Amazon seller inbox. Since Amazon allows you to use your email to respond to customers instead of creating a particular kind of email address, you can use this app.

- Flashback Express: it can only be used on Windows, unfortunately. It can be used to quickly capture and annotate your voice and then upload the video on your screen. This can be used to communicate something that is in your store. Or deliver something that is on your screen to a colleague or your occasional customer. This makes the message more personal than ever, and it can be the best way to explain something to your customers in an easier manner, and it can make you quite popular among other clients. It can bring you more customers as well.

- Unroll.me: There are dozens upon dozens of emails that you receive from a seller on a daily basis about different offers that you are going to get from Amazon. The difference between having this app and not having it, is you are required to need to keep clicking delete or unsubscribe manually.

This app allows you to unsubscribe from those emails or offers that you do not want to have in bulk. There are tutorials online that you can use to help you navigate through the app with ease.

Time saving hacks: To save your time as a salesperson when screening your items and scanning them, you can use the $0.00 buy cost to help you when browsing for items mainly in the app's field "Buy$." The time that you spend typing at the expense of the item is deducted since it costs nothing! You can use a calculator to subtract the actual buying price of the item from the profit price and decide on whether you will purchase the item or you will forgo it.

At times, it is not necessary for you to do the math of whether you will get to buy the product; all you have got to do is check if the price you are buying the item is higher or lower than the price of the profit you are bound to make.

An example would be if the cost of the head gear is at $12.99 and the profit you are required to make is at $9.99; you will not buy the item since it costs more than what you are going to get from the profit.

Other ways of reducing the scanning process are through downloading the Amazon 1Button app. It is an extension from chrome that shows you the price of the item you require, and it does the searching or looking or scanning for you.

An instance would be when looking for game boards; the app will let you know if the game is sold on Amazon and the price of the game. This saves you the trouble of going through Amazon trying to find the game and if it is even available and the price as well.

Keep in mind that not always does the search engine provide the results that you are looking for and at times the items might not even be available or found.

Make sure you invest in the best supplies you possibly can get your hands on. There are the common denominators of supplies that most Amazon sellers have in their arsenal and use them. Most of them swear by these items and can attest to their immense help when carrying out their daily sales.

Have a business credit card and checking account: in your daily life, you have a personal credit card that you use mainly to buy your items and spend it as you wish. You also, most definitely (if not, get one ASAP!) keep track of your expenses and savings as well.

You can have a software tracking app on your every expense charged to your credit card, be it personal or business. For the Amazon FBA, you need to have a business credit card and checking account to keep track of what you are spending on and where your money goes. This card and account need to be different from your credit and checking account.

You can use Quickbooks as a way to keep track of your personal and business accounts and credit cards. The app allows you to:
- Keep track of what you have spent
- Know how much you owe your credit card and
- Where you shop at

Run your business like a business: With this being your business, even if you are running it at your house, you need to run it like one. To make shipping easier, create your shipping and prepping station.

It doesn't have to be anything fancy or too elaborate, get a small table and lean it against a wall. Have drawers (they could be colored or whatever pattern you prefer) close by that house all your poly bags, shipping tapes, scissors, liquid fluid and any other necessary appliance that you need to wrap your shipping items and put them in your box.

Having or creating order in your house can help you run your business very smoothly. The station will help you reduce the time spent running around looking for scissors, the shipping tape or trying to figure out where to lay your merchandise at so that you can work.

The area around your working station can function as your prepping station, where you gather all your necessary items, put them together before you move to your working station to put the final touches on your product before shipping them off to your customer.

The station can act as a studio of some sort. When you have laid out your items on the table, you can take a picture of the items and use them for your store on Amazon. The pictures can be edited; changing the color in the background to pure white t put it on the product listing images

section of your site. You can learn
more on how on Photoshop
Elements on this site
http://www.secondhalfdreams.co
m/4202/how-to-create-an-
image-that-meets-amazons-
requirements/

*Know a good deal when you see
one*: While finding a niche is
important to the long-term
strength of your FBA store, the
most important rule of FBA is that
if you can make a profit on it then
you should sell it. As such,
regardless of what the product is if
you find yourself staring at a sale
that is 75 percent off or more then
there is always going to be room
enough there for you to make a
profit on the item. The key to not
putting too much work into this
type of passive income is to always
passively be on the lookout for
good deals and be ready and able
to jump on them when you see
them because the best deals are
never going to stick around for
very long.

Care about your seller rating: Just because you letting Amazon do most of the heavy lifting doesn't mean that you can let your store run on autopilot. Specifically, you are going to want to be aware of your seller rating and do  everything you can to keep it as high as possible. If you sell faulty merchandise or items that fall apart quickly then this number will drop rapidly which means you will want to consider all the costs of a particular product, not just what you pay to take direct ownership of the product. What's more, if you make a habit of selling unreliable items then Amazon can drop you from the service for hurting their image, something that you will obviously want to avoid at all costs.

Consider each purchase carefully: The best online retail arbitrage products are those that are heavily discounted, irrespective of the type of product in question. As a general rule, if you find anything, literally anything that is marked down 75 percent from its original price, then you can likely find a way to sell it for a profit online; whether it is worth it is another question. Another great choice are items that you can purchase in bulk cheaply now, before waiting for natural scarcity to set in six months or so down the line when your investment will pay off in spades.

A great example of this are toys you can purchase from a dollar store that are based on properties that are never going to go out of style such as Disney properties like Princesses, Star Wars or Marvel superheroes. Many of these products are only ever sold at dollar stores which means that after the initial stock dries up there will be thousands of parents out there looking for character specific merchandise that their child has not consumed yet. If you aren't interested in waiting, you can instead group a number of themed items together, knock a fraction of the total profit off and sell the total as a true bargain.

For example, if you purchase five Disney Princess puzzles for a total of $5, knowing that each typically sells for $5 on Amazon, then you can sell all five for $20, still have the group seen as the value, and even make more than a 50 percent profit on the transaction. If you pursue this course of action, you are going to generate a unique UPC code for the group of products, though you can use the same UPC code for multiple groups if applicable.

Don't forget about social media: The most essential social media for any company or brand to have is Facebook. Pretty much everybody uses Facebook, and having an active Facebook page is absolutely essential. Do whatever you can in order to build your Facebook fan base. Your posts aren't always going to get a ton of traction, but any traction and any traffic matters... plus, if you make

a really good post, you're going to
see a lot of traffic come from it
naturally. That's just how it works
with social media.

You're also going to want to
consider getting Twitter and
Instagram. These aren't quite as
popular as Facebook and are more
geared towards people in the 16 to
30 crowd, so if your niche aims at
people who are older, then you
may not have as much success on
these. However, having a popular
following on these networks can
make a lot of difference for you as
a company if you follow through
with it appropriately and make a
lot of posts.

Finally, you're going to want to set
up a Snapchat. Snapchat is
potentially one of the best
marketing platforms because
unlike other forms of social media,
where only a portion of your
followers can see your content
without specifically going to your
page, a story on Snapchat is visible
to all of your followers. If you have
a particularly visually appealing

niche, Snapchat can be a great way to show people what you're up to and what's up next on your blog. This extra traffic and these return users will, in turn, lead to a big return on your affiliate marketing products.

Chapter 6: Settle in for the Long-Term

After learning the basics of shipping and making a few sales, there are some things need to be taken into consideration as they are essential to ensuring your business will remain successful for years to come. The traction of your business refers to the progress that your firm, especially a start-up business and the progress it is making as it grows; is the speed slow or fast or is the pace at which it develops as expected?

It is often difficult to get your business to kick off running and selling which in turn bring you profits and raises the cash you require to either repay debts and clear with the bank or start finding new ways of improving the business. The resources that are needed to get your business up and running might not be available, or you are short a few coins, but your reputation might be at stake if you do not keep above the curve of the business and the competition as well.

Understand your audience: As long as you are fully aware of your product and theoretically who may be ready to buy it, then you are already well on your way to understanding your audience. Likewise, sending out customer surveys is a great way to get the basics of the demographics that you are looking for. Once you have a general outline that represents your customer base the next step is to go deep and determine who their social media influencers are. These can be either YouTube or other social media personalities who are extremely popular in certain demographics.

Once you understand who these people are, you will want to consume a fair bit of their content to get an idea of the types of references they make and the types of slang they use. If you want your customers to connect with your brand you are going to want them to feel like they are embracing one of their own. Once you have appropriated the appropriate culture, the next step is to send your products directly to these influencers in hopes that they will like what you have sent and then ideally use or talk about it at some point down the line. While this might initially seem expensive, this should be considered a marketing expense and its results can be extremely lucrative.

It is important to not leave Instagram influencers out of the equation either as recent studies indicate that items that were positively rated by top influencers were directly correlated to an increase of sales of nearly 30 percent, what's more, nearly all of those customers were new to the site which means this type of exposure can be extremely influential. When it comes to creating a buzz around your brand, this type of marketing will give your store a grass roots feel that is extremely popular among the demographics that are the most likely to use the internet to buy goods and services on a regular basis. To find more information on popular influences, Websta.com can provide lists of the most commonly searched for usernames for Instagram and other sites, it also allows you to search hashtags.

Ask for customer feedback: Many FBA sellers underestimate the importance of getting feedback from customers but it is crucial to ensuring your business survives in the long-term. Amazon states that customers are allowed to leave comments on the orders that have been transacted by Amazon, for sellers to view. This is the same for merchant-fulfilled orders.

The FBA orders can work wonders for you as an entrepreneur. The sales can hit the roof and also this can be a way for you to increase your reputation as a seller, even though you are new in the market.

About the customer's feedback, this is a way to conclude a client's experience on a positive note:
- Communication with the seller
- Packaging of the product(s)
- Shipping process
- Customer service
- Dispute resolution- which has to be on point.

Amazon, if not always, helps an average seller to have the best shipping and packaging services that are equal to professional dealers. This is if you are participating in the FBA program.

With FBA orders, the same as any other orders run through or by Amazon; when customers are not satisfied with the product they purchased or with any of the fulfillment services that are provided by Amazon, the feedback received, Amazon will strike through.

If anything does go wrong, there is a chance that the problem mainly isn't with you but with Amazon. The FBA solicitation process value increases so does the tracking changes that your feedback score provides.

You have the option of tracking your comments manually. You need to do this as often as you possibly can. To do this; bookmark the Amazon Feedback Manager section in your Seller Central dashboards. Ratings daily may vary considerably all dependent on the volume of your orders. The more orders you get, the number of ratings will increase as well. It could get to the point of you going through new feedback for hours in a span of three to four months.

You could also use FeedbackFive that is an automatic way of looking at your feedback. How this works is there will be alerts that will notify you of negative, neutral or new feedback.

You can receive the comment in either mail or text form. This is less stressful for you; since you don't have to spend hours going through your dashboard to see if there is any new feedback.

To clear any disputes with your customer that is your fault, make sure you resolve the issue as fast as you can by taking the necessary steps to do so. After, then and only then can you ask for a removal of the feedback. In case you believe it is Amazon's fault, you can request for them to remove the negative feedback.

Set the right goals

The SMART system is a way of focusing your time on goals that will create the maximum amount of benefit possible. Goals should always have a timeframe, be relevant, achievable, measurable and specific. Regardless of what you are trying to achieve, applying the SMART test is a good way to make sure you are getting the most out of any effort you put in.

Specific: It is important to always have a specific, clear goal in mind whenever you set out to accomplish something new. The foggier the goal, the easier it will be for your mind to come up with excuses to do something more immediately satisfying instead. Having something specific in mind instead gives you something to focus on when your mind starts putting forth excuses. Know your goal and focus on it when times get tough and you will find it easier to power through the right way.

If you aren't sure if your goal is
specific enough, run through the
5Ws and H: who, what, where,
why, when and how. If your goal is

specific enough that you can determine who will be involved, what will be accomplished, where it will be accomplished, why you are doing it, when you will start working on it and how you will see it through then you are likely on the right track.

Measurable: Appropriate goals are those which can be clearly defined between a set of points, one which indicates success and the other which indicates failure. Especially when you are first starting out, it is important to always choose goals that will allow you to clearly know when you are drifting off track. Measuring your progress will ensure that you are able to keep up the good work as you will know that you are hitting required deadlines and meeting all of your due dates with ease.

Attainable: Quality goals are those which are realistically attainable. As previously stated, it is important to always stick with attainable goals, especially at first. In this early state trying and failing, may be worse than not trying at all. This doesn't mean you must always pick goals that are easy, however, easy goals typically lead to fewer rewards. They are fine at first, but eventually, you will want to choose goals that are attainable through additional hard work and planning as they tend to be significantly more rewarding in the long run.

Relevant: Choosing a specific, measurable, attainable goal is meaningless if what you have chosen isn't relevant to your current situation. It is important for the goals you choose, specifically your first few to be as relevant and there fulfilling when they are completed as possible. You are working on building new neural pathways and effort that doesn't directly correlate to reward gives your brain nothing to associate together which makes the entire exercise moot.

Likewise, it is important to pick an initial goal that will easily fit into your current routine. Early goals have few habits to fall back on, add part of them to each day's to-do list and complete it in chunks slowly but surely. Make a habit out of completing part of the task and you will slowly but surely be able to count on yourself to complete more and more complicated scenarios. Like with everything in life, practice makes perfect.

Timely: A goal is not truly a goal unless it has a clearly defined end point. Having a time limit will make it more likely for you to focus on the goal at hand as something that you should work to accomplish right now as opposed to something you are planning on working to accomplish eventually. The timeframe that you choose for success should not be overly ambitious, while at the same time not feeling lax. The point is you should feel pressured to hurry up and get to work, so set a timeframe that you will have to hustle slightly to succeed.

Become an authority

In many situations, the word expert and the word authority are often used interchangeably; this is not the case with online marketing, however, as being an authority is everything and being an expert is much worse than simply getting second place. In this case, an expert is someone who knows a lot about a certain niche while an authority is the person that all of the experts agree is the first stop for information on a given niche. To put it another way, authorities aren't authorities because they say they are, they are authorities because when they make declarations in regards to their niche of choice, other people listen.

The benefits of being an authority in relation to a given niche, are much the same as any other authority figure when you speak everyone will listen. This is because those who know you are an authority will expect that you know what you are talking about in any given situation, after all, you must know best. It doesn't take much of an imagination to see how this can directly translate into additional sales when given the proper push. If you can reach the status of authority for your niche you will be able to set the tone for the entire niche as well as have a legion of loyal followers willing to defend everything you say.

When it comes to marketing for your online business or website, it is important to have a healthy social media presence as well as a firm grasp of the importance of SEO if you want to reach out and find new revenue streams. If you also spend time slowly building a reputation as an authority in a given niche, then you will be able to rest easy the revenue streams will come to you instead.

Do your homework: The first step to writing content that will help you to see as though you are an authority in your niche is going to be difficult for some people and easy for others depending on their ability to get online and do the research that being an authority in a chosen niche requires. Put another way, you need to learn enough to know what it is you are talking about in any situation you might find yourself in regarding your niche.

Not to worry, this isn't something that is going to take you years to master as it is perfectly acceptable to focus on a single aspect of your niche to the exclusion of all others. Not only does this have the benefit of ensuring that you will actually get to use the information you are learning at a point in the near future, but it will also allow you to differentiate yourself from any other authorities in the niche without having to actively go head to head with them.

Once you do get to work, it is important to do more than simply becoming familiar with the

Wikipedia page on the topic, it means going to the sources that you can find connected to that Wikipedia page and then tracking down there sources as well. You will then want to do this again, and again and again until you can honestly say that you have left no stone unturned. It will unavoidably require lots of hard work and effort, though the results will certainly pay for themselves in the long run.

While you are working your way through this process you may also find it helpful to create a starter guide as if you were writing for someone who is completely unfamiliar with whatever part of your niche you are working at becoming an authority in. While putting together a study guide for a topic that you are not yet terribly familiar with might seem like a poor choice, the fact of the matter is that absorbing the complicated topics you are studying and breaking them down in such a way that anyone can understand will help take the content from something you've learned to something you can easily explain, which is what you will be spending a lot of time doing through your blog.

Limit yourself: When it comes to becoming an authority in something that your niche cares about, it is important to set realistic goals for yourself in order to ensure that you are undertaking a reasonable goal. This means rather than setting out to become an authority on absolutely everything that is going on with your niche, you content yourself to learning everything about a vertical slice of it instead. The more focused your research is, the more breathing room you will have and the easier it will be to get a handle on just what you are taking on. Remember, a jack of all trades is a master of none.

Know your competition: Just as there are going to be major players in your niche that you did research on before committing to a specific goal, it is important to know who your competition is in the authority space surrounding your niche. Finding this person shouldn't be hard, all you need to do is search for your niche on Google and look for the names that come up most frequently. Once this is done, you will then need to decide if you would be better off trying to dethrone them or taking on a subsection of the niche instead. Regardless of how entrenched this other person is, there is always going to be room for another authority in a niche, you may just need to go above and beyond when it comes to determining just where that room actually is.

Create a guide: While it might seem like an odd recommendation for you to write a guide while you are still learning, you will be surprised at how effective of a learning tool it can actually be. Not only will this result in valuable content that can be used in multiple ways later on, but it will also ensure that you are extremely comfortable with the material in general, which will help to get it into your long-term memory as quickly as possible. What's more, you will find that you learn the underlying concepts more fully when you need to rely on the relevant information in its most basic form.

Grow your reach: While it should be easy for your actual customers to think of you as a credible source at this point if you want to truly become an authority figure you are going to need to branch out substantially. Your goal during this phase should be to spread throughout the niche as completely as possible to the point that whenever anyone who is interested in the niche interacts with it, they can't help but see your name. This means you are going to want to spend time on forums talking about the niche and answering the questions that other people might have. Whenever you are able to do so successfully, you can then credit the information to your website, link included.

You will also want to join social media groups for sellers and bloggers in the niche so that you can get to know your competition as well. Not only will this allow you to get an inside look at their strengths and weaknesses, nothing says you are an authority figure like getting a guest spot on someone else's blog. As anyone who runs a blog can tell you, coming up with enough unique content every week to remain relevant can be a serious chore which is why, assuming you have proven yourself to be a reliable source of information in the community, any blogger should be happy to allow you to run a guest blog.

Once you have access to your competition's customers, you are going to want to do your best to take full advantage of the situation. First, you are going to want to ensure that the content you create is cream of the crop, buy a professional post online if you have to, just provide something that people are going to be interested in reading. End the post on a natural stopping point but offer those who are interested in more a follow up on your own site, link included. Finally, seal the deal by providing a coupon code in the post that is good for a serious discount on your own products as well. People will come to your site assuming you are an authority and additional conversions will follow.

Make friends: While utilizing other authorities and experts for what they can do for you will certainly help you to become a more well-known authority in your chosen field, it is important to not let the cutthroat world of online content marketing make you into someone who is only out for themselves. Having a reputation of being a good person, someone that other respected members of the niche community respect is almost as beneficial as being considered an authority. Likewise, you can recommend products and services that you don't even sell which will make everything else that you recommend look sincerer as a result.

This tactic will also lead more of your target audience to feel a stronger connection with you because a basic part of human psychology is that we like people better when they start by putting their worst foot forward. This is a disarming trait which makes it easier to trust the person in question as it is clear that they really have nothing to hide. As such, your relationship with both the other content creators, as well as your subscribers and your target audience will be strengthened as a result. Finally, your target audience will appreciate the fact that you are committed to telling the truth about a given product or service even when it isn't obviously in your best interest to do so.

Instead of just taking a guest spot on another site, reciprocate, talk about the cool things that other people are writing about or doing and encourage your target audience to broaden their horizons. Not only will this help to strengthen your place in the community and lead to more reciprocation, but it will also show that you are confident enough in what you are doing to not be threatened by other presences in the same space. After all, if you are an authority then you have nothing to fear from those who are simply experts.

Create email blasts: Once you have started gathering a bit of a following, you are going to want to capitalize on that fact by creating a mailing list where you provide even more free content to those who are looking for all of your wisdom that they can get. You can easily utilize the contact form that should already be on your site for this purpose, and even if you aren't ready to start an email blast quite yet, it is important to try and gather as many email addresses as possible for when you ultimately have a use for them.

Email blasts are primarily used as a marketing device, though doing so needs to be handled delicately for the best results. You are going to want to typically stick to a margin that leans heavily towards legitimate content and lightly on advertising if you want your open rates to remain high overtime. As long as you don't overdo it, however, then this can be a great way to get a target audience to trust you to look at things you want them to buy.

You can then use something called an autoresponder to send them new links to products you are promoting automatically once the information has been collected. Consider the following tips to create the type of autoresponder messages that get the response you need to start seeing real results in the long term:

When setting up an autoresponder message, you will want to pick an average of 5 products that do not directly compete with one another but are still clearly related.

In addition to sending out a new unsolicited email every 4 days, you need to track the emails that you do send out and determine how many people opened each email and how many actually bought something because of it. As you gain more information to work off of you can more specifically target your emails to have a better success rate among your target audience.

When it comes to understanding what you can do to ensure that your autoresponder emails are opened, the first thing you will want to do is to send emails from your name directly. Assuming you have connected your name with your brand, opening an email from you should be akin to opening an email from anyone else your readers know. Outside of that, there are several important guidelines to consider to ensure readers keep opening your unsolicited emails for years to come.

35 percent of your subscribers will open any email with the right subject line. This means your subject line should be short and sweet, no more than 10 words but no fewer than 6. The subject line should imply useful content related to the niche in question. This ensures you are at least including something you know your audience should, in theory, be interested in.

When it comes to finding useful content that you know your audience is interested in, the best place to start is with the posts that have gotten the greatest number of views previously and expand on that information. If you expect your subscribers to open content that they know is going to try and sell them something you must deliver on your promise for quality useful content every single time.

Conversions by source: If despite your authority in your niche you find that your conversions by source aren't where you would like them to be, then there are a few things you will want to ensure you are doing properly before moving on to more advanced tactics. The first thing you will want to consider is the HTML email you are using. If it is comprised of one large picture, then if that picture can't be displayed for any reason then you are cutting out a large portion of your customer base. Go back to the testing phase and ensure everything is working in as many different scenarios as possible and see if things improve.

Additionally, your conversions might be down because you are offering up too many choices and your subscribers are experiencing choice paralysis. Especially as your focus has shifted from just an email newsletter to a blog and being seen as an authority in the niche as a whole it is natural for your newsletter to pick up bloat along the way. Slice and dice, shake it up and maybe try something new, your conversions could simply be down because fatigue has set in. You may even want to stop publishing a newsletter for a short period of time, just so people can realize they miss your expertise. Then, when you come back new and improved, your conversion rate should naturally jump as a result.

Conclusion

Thanks for making it through to the end of *AMAZON FBA MASTERY COACHING*, let's hope it was informative and able to provide you with all of the tools you need to achieve your goals, whatever it is that they may be. Just because you've finished this book doesn't mean there is nothing left to learn on the topic, and expanding your horizons is the only way to find the mastery you seek.

Now that you have made it to the end of this book, you hopefully have an understanding of how to get started creating your own passive income stream with FBA, as well as a strategy or two, or three, that you are anxious to try for the first time. Before you go ahead and start giving it your all, however, it is important that you have realistic expectations as to the level of success you should expect in the near future.

While it is perfectly true that some people experience serious success right out of the gate, it is an unfortunate fact of life that they are the exception rather than the rule. What this means is that you should expect to experience something of a learning curve, especially when you are first figuring out what works for you. This is perfectly normal, however, and if you persevere you will come out the other side better because of it. Instead of getting your hopes up to an unrealistic degree, you should think of your time spent building your passive income stream as a marathon rather than a sprint which means that slow and steady will win the race every single time.

The next step is to stop reading and to start doing whatever is required of you in order to ensure that yourself and those you care about will be on good financial grounds and stability. If you find that you still need help getting started you will likely have better results by creating a schedule that you hope to follow including personal milestones and practical applications for various parts of the tasks as well as the overall process of acquiring the life changing knowledge and experiences.

In this light, studies show that complex tasks that are broken down into individual pieces, including individual targets, have a much greater chance of being completed when compared to something that has a general need of being completed but no real time table for doing so. Even though it would seem silly, go ahead and set your own deadlines for completion, complete with indicators of success and failure. After you have successfully completed all of your required milestones, you will be glad you took that former step

Once you have finished the initial process it is important to understand that it is just that, only part of a larger plan of preparation. Your best chances for overall success will come by taking the time to learn as many vital skills as possible. Only by using your prepared status as a springboard to greater profit margins will you be able to truly rest soundly knowing that you are finally taking the right steps into realizing your financial balance and stability, not to mention prosperity.

Finally, if you found this book useful in any way, a review on Amazon is always appreciated!

JONATHAN FITZPATRICK

SIGN UP

Visit my website www. *jonathanfitzpatrickauthor.com* and enter your email address in the sign-up form to receive free exclusive bonus contents related to the updates of this book and find out everything about Jonathan Fitzpatrick's new publications, launch offers and other exclusive promotions!

Made in the USA
Middletown, DE
28 June 2019